COLLINS
ENGLISH
NURSERY
RHYMES
FOR YOUNG LEARNERS

English
for Children

COLLINS ELT
London and Glasgow

Collins ELT
8 Grafton St
London W1X 3LA

© William Collins Sons & Company Ltd 1981
© ELT edition, Collins ELT 1986

10 9 8 7 6 5 4 3 2 1

ISBN Book: 0 00 370221 9
ISBN Cassette: 0 00 370222 7

Cover design by Gina Smart
Published by William Collins plc
Printed in Hong Kong by
Wing King Tong Ltd

Contents

Let's begin

Out goes the rat,
Out goes the cat,
Out goes the lady   With the big green hat.
Y, O, U, spells you;
O, U, T, spells out!

Dip dip dip,
My blue ship,
Sailing on the water,
Like a cup and saucer.
Dip dip dip,
You're not It.

Eenie, meenie, minie, mo,
Catch a tiger by the toe,
If he hollers, let him go,
Eenie, meenie, minie, mo.

Ickle ockle, blue bockle,
    Fishes in the sea,
If you want a pretty maid,
    Please choose me.

One potato, two potato,
Three potato, four;
Five potato, six potato,
Seven potato, MORE.

One to ten, and then again

One, two, three,
I love coffee,
And Billy loves tea,
How good you be,
One, two, three,
I love coffee,
And Billy loves tea.

One, two, three, four, five,
Once I caught a fish alive,
Six, seven, eight, nine, ten,
Then I let it go again.
Why did you let it go?
Because it bit my finger so.
Which finger did it bite?
The little finger on the right.

One, two,
    Buckle my shoe;
Three, four,
    Knock at the door;
Five, six,
    Pick up sticks;
Seven, eight,
    Lay them straight;
Nine, ten,
    A big fat hen;
Eleven, twelve,
    Dig and delve;
Thirteen, fourteen,
    Maids a-courting;
Fifteen, sixteen,
    Maids in the kitchen;
Seventeen, eighteen,
    Maids in waiting;
Nineteen, twenty,
    My plate's empty.

Nursery days

Bye, baby bunting,
Daddy's gone a-hunting,
Gone to get a rabbit skin
To wrap the baby bunting in.

Pat-a-cake, pat-a-cake, baker's man,
Bake me a cake as fast as you can;
Pat it and prick it, and mark it with B,
Put it in the oven for Baby and me.

Dance to your daddy,
  My little babby,
Dance to your daddy,
  My little lamb.

You shall have a fishy
  In a little dishy,
You shall have a fishy
  When the boat comes in.

You shall have an apple,
  You shall have a plum,
You shall have a rattle-basket
  When your daddy comes home.

Hush-a-bye, baby, on the tree top,
When the wind blows, the cradle will rock;
When the bough breaks, the cradle will fall,
And down will come baby, cradle and all.

How many days has my baby to play?
Saturday, Sunday, Monday,
Tuesday, Wednesday, Thursday, Friday,
Saturday, Sunday, Monday.
Hop away, skip away,
My baby wants to play;
My baby wants to play every day!

Nonsensical rhymes

Hey diddle, diddle,
The cat and the fiddle,
The cow jumped over the moon;
The little dog laughed
To see such sport,
And the dish ran away with
the spoon.

Rub-a-dub-dub,
Three men in a tub,
And how do you think they got there?
The butcher, the baker,
The candlestick-maker,
They all jumped out of a rotten potato,
'Twas enough to make a man stare.

A man in the wilderness, he asked me,
How many strawberries grow in the sea.
I answered him, as I thought good,
As many red herrings as swim in the wood.

Humpty Dumpty sat on a wall,
Humpty Dumpty had a great fall;
All the King's horses
And all the King's men
Couldn't put Humpty together again.

Owen Moore went away,
Owing more than he could pay.
Owen Moore came back next day,
Owing more.

Hoddley, poddley, puddle and fogs,
Cats are to marry the poodle dogs;
Cats in blue jackets and dogs in red hats,
What will become of the mice and the rats?

Mother, may I go out to swim?
    Yes, my darling daughter.
Hang your clothes on a hickory limb
    And don't go near the water.

In the city,
in the street

Up and down the City Road,
In and out the Eagle,
That's the way the money goes,
Pop goes the weasel!

London Bridge is falling down,
Falling down, falling down;
London Bridge is falling down,
My fair lady.

We must build it up again,
Up again, up again;
We must build it up again,
My fair lady.

Half a pound of tuppenny rice,
Half a pound of treacle,
Mix it up and make it nice,
Pop goes the weasel!

Every night when I go out
The monkey's on the table;
Take a stick and knock it off,
Pop goes the weasel!

Oranges and lemons,
　　Say the bells of St Clement's.
You owe me five farthings,
　　Say the bells of St Martin's.
When will you pay me?
　　Say the bells of Old Bailey.
When I grow rich,
　　Say the bells of Shoreditch.
When will that be?
　　Say the bells of Stepney.
I'm sure I don't know,
　　Says the Great Bell of Bow.

Sally go round the sun,
Sally go round the moon,
Sally go round the chimney-pots
On a Saturday afternoon.

13

Mary had a Little Lamb

Mary had a little lamb,
  Its fleece was white as snow;
And everywhere that Mary went
  The lamb was sure to go.

It followed her to school one day,
  That was against the rule;
It made the children laugh and play
  To see a lamb at school.

And so the teacher turned it out,
　But still it lingered near,
And waited patiently about
　Till Mary did appear.

Why does the lamb love Mary so?
　The eager children cry;
Why, Mary loves the lamb, you know,
　The teacher did reply.

Cherry stone rhymes

Who shall I marry?

Tinker,
Tailor,
Soldier,
Sailor,
Rich man,
Poor man,
Beggar man,
Thief.

When will it be?

This year,
Next year,
Sometime,
Never.

Where shall I marry?

Church,
Chapel,
Cathedral,
Abbey.

And the ring?

Gold,
Silver,
Copper,
Brass.

How shall I get there?

Coach,
Carriage,
Wheelbarrow,
Dustcart.

What shall I wear?

Silk,
Satin,
Cotton,
Rags.

And where shall we live happily ever after?

Big house,
Little house,
Pig sty,
Barn.

What's for dinner?

Davy Davy Dumpling,
Boil him in the pot;
Sugar him and butter him,
And eat him while he's hot.

Polly put the kettle on,
Polly put the kettle on,
Polly put the kettle on,
We'll all have tea.

Sukey take it off again,
Sukey take it off again,
Sukey take it off again,
They've all gone away.

Pease porridge hot,
Pease porridge cold,
Pease porridge in the pot
Nine days old.
Some like it hot,
Some like it cold,
Some like it in the pot
Nine days old.

Little Miss Muffet
Sat on a tuffet,
Eating her curds and whey;
There came a big spider,
Who sat down beside her
And frightened Miss Muffet away.

Little Tommy Tucker
Sings for his supper:
What shall we give him?
White bread and butter.
How shall he cut it
Without e'er a knife?
How will he be married
Without e'er a wife?

Jack Sprat could eat no fat,
His wife could eat no lean,
And so between them both, you see,
They licked the platter clean.

21

Jack and Jill

Jack and Jill
Went up the hill,
To fetch a pail of water;
Jack fell down,
And broke his crown,
And Jill came tumbling after.

Then up Jack got,
And home did trot,
As fast as he could caper;
He went to bed,
To mend his head,
With vinegar and brown paper.

Rain, rain, go away!

Blow, wind, blow!
And go, mill, go!
That the miller may grind his corn;
That the baker may take it,
And into bread make it,
And bring us a loaf in the morn.

Rain on the green grass,
And rain on the tree,
Rain on the house-top,
But not on me.

March winds and April showers
Bring forth May flowers.

Ipsey Wipsey spider
  Climbing up the spout;
Down came the rain
  And washed the spider out:
Out came the sunshine
  And dried up all the rain;
Ipsey Wipsey spider
  Climbing up again.

A sunshiny shower
Won't last half an hour.

Rain, rain, go away,
Come again another day,
Little Johnny wants to play.

Lazy days

Ladybird, ladybird,
　Fly away home,
Your house is on fire
　And your children are gone;
All except one
　And that's little Ann
And she has crept under
　The frying pan.

A diller, a dollar,
A ten o'clock scholar,
What makes you come so soon?
You used to come at ten o'clock,
But now you come at noon.

Buttercups and daisies,
　Oh what pretty flowers,
Coming in the springtime
　To tell of sunny hours.
While the trees are leafless,
　While the fields are bare,
Buttercups and daisies
　Spring up everywhere.

The cock's on the wood pile
    Blowing his horn,
The bull's in the barn
    A-threshing the corn,
The maids in the meadow
    Are making the hay,
The ducks in the river
    Are swimming away.

A swarm of bees in May
Is worth a load of hay;
A swarm of bees in June
Is worth a silver spoon;
A swarm of bees in July
Is not worth a fly.

Little Boy Blue,
    Come blow your horn,
The sheep's in the meadow,
    The cow's in the corn.
Where is the boy
    Who looks after the sheep?
He's under a haycock
    Fast asleep.
Will you wake him?
    No, not I,
For if I do,
    He's sure to cry.

27

Playtime

I'm the king of the castle,
Get down you dirty rascal.

Finders keepers,
Losers weepers.

Lucy Locket lost her pocket,
Kitty Fisher found it;
Not a penny was there in it,
Only ribbon round it.

Tell tale tit,
Your tongue shall be split
And all the little puppy dogs,
Shall have a little bit!

Here am I,
  Little Jumping Joan;
When nobody's with me
  I'm all alone.

I'll sing you a song,
Nine verses long,
  For a pin;
Three and three are six,
And three are nine;
You are a fool,
  And the pin is mine.

Strange folk

Goosey, goosey gander,
    Whither shall I wander?
Upstairs and downstairs
    And in my lady's chamber.
There I met an old man
    Who would not say his prayers,
I took him by the left leg
    And threw him down the stairs.

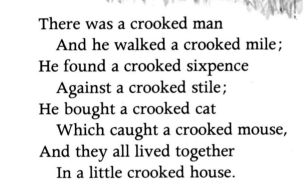

There was a crooked man
    And he walked a crooked mile;
He found a crooked sixpence
    Against a crooked stile;
He bought a crooked cat
    Which caught a crooked mouse,
And they all lived together
    In a little crooked house.

Peter, Peter, pumpkin eater,
Had a wife and couldn't keep her;
He put her in a pumpkin shell
And there he kept her very well.

Peter, Peter, pumpkin eater,
Had another, and didn't love her;
Peter learned to read and spell,
And then he loved her very well.

Mrs. Mason bought a basin,
Mrs. Tyson said, What a nice 'un,
What did it cost? said Mrs. Frost,
Half a crown, said Mrs. Brown,
Did it indeed, said Mrs. Reed,
It did for certain, said Mrs. Burton.
Then Mrs. Nix up to her tricks
Threw the basin on the bricks.

There was an old woman tossed up in a basket,
Seventeen times as high as the moon;
Where she was going I couldn't but ask it,
For in her hand she carried a broom.
Old woman, old woman, old woman, quoth I,
Where are you going to up so high?
To brush the cobwebs off the sky!
May I go with you? Aye, by-and-by.

Doctor Foster went to Gloucester
In a shower of rain;
He stepped in a puddle,
Right up to his middle,
And never went there again.

Soldier, Soldier

Oh, soldier, soldier, will you marry me,
    With your musket, fife, and drum?
Oh no, pretty maid, I cannot marry you,
    For I have no coat to put on.

Then away she went
    To her grandfather's chest,
And bought him one of the very very best,
    And the soldier put it on.

Oh, soldier, soldier, will you marry me,
    With your musket, fife, and drum?
Oh no, pretty maid, I cannot marry you,
    For I have no socks to put on.

Then away she went
    To her grandfather's chest,
And bought him a pair of the very very best,
    And the soldier put them on.

Oh, soldier, soldier, will you marry me,
    With your musket, fife, and drum?
Oh no, pretty maid, I cannot marry you,
    For I have no shoes to put on.

Then away she went
    To her grandfather's chest,
And bought him a pair of the very very best,
    And the soldier put them on.

Oh, soldier, soldier, will you marry me,
   With your musket, fife, and drum?
Oh no, pretty maid, I cannot marry you,
   For I have no hat to put on.

Then away she went
   To her grandfather's chest,
And bought him one of the very very best,
   And the soldier put it on.

Oh, soldier, soldier, will you marry me,
   With your musket fife, and drum?
Oh no, pretty maid, I cannot marry you,
   For I have a wife at home.

Kings and Queens

Hector Protector was dressed all in green;
Hector Protector was sent to the Queen.
　　The Queen did not like him,
　　No more did the King;
So Hector Protector was sent back again.

Old King Cole
　Was a merry old soul,
And a merry old soul was he;
　He called for his pipe,
　And he called for his bowl,
And he called for his fiddlers three.

Every fiddler he had a fiddle,
And a very fine fiddle had he;
　Oh, there's none so rare
　As can compare
With King Cole and his fiddlers
　three.

The Queen of Hearts
    She made some tarts,
All on a summer's day;
    The Knave of Hearts
    He stole those tarts,
And took them clean away.

    The King of Hearts
    Called for the tarts,
And beat the knave full sore;
    The Knave of Hearts
    Brought back the tarts,
And vowed he'd steal no more.

I had a little nut tree,
    Nothing would it bear
But a silver nutmeg
    And a golden pear;
The king of Spain's daughter
    Came to visit me,
And all for the sake
    Of my little nut tree.
I skipped over water,
    I danced over sea,
And all the birds in the air
    Couldn't catch me.

Lavender's blue, diddle, diddle,
    Lavender's green;
When I am king, diddle, diddle,
    You shall be queen.

Bow-wow
says the dog

I had a dog
    Whose name was Buff,
I sent him for
    A bag of snuff;
He broke the bag
    And spilled the stuff,
And that was all
    My penny's worth.

Bow-wow, says the dog,
Mew, mew, says the cat,
Grunt, grunt, goes the hog,
And squeak goes the rat.
Tu-whu, says the owl,
Caw, caw, says the crow,
Quack, quack, says the duck,
And what cuckoos say you know.

I had a dog and his name was Dandy,
His tail was long and his legs were bandy,
His eyes were brown and his coat was sandy,
The best in the world was my dog Dandy.

Oh where, oh where has my little dog gone?
Oh where, oh where can he be?
With his ears cut short and his tail cut long,
Oh where, oh where is he?

Hark, hark,
    The dogs do bark,
The beggars are coming to town;
    Some in rags,
    And some in jags,
And one in a velvet gown.

Join hands!

Poor Mary lies a-weeping, a-weeping, a-weeping,
Poor Mary lies a-weeping, on a bright summer's day!

Oh, why is she a-weeping, a-weeping, a-weeping?
Oh, why is she a-weeping, on a bright summer's day?

She's weeping for her true love, her true love, her true love,
She's weeping for her true love, on a bright summer's day.

On the carpet she must kneel,
Till the grass grows in the field,
Stand up now, upon your feet,
Choose the one you love so sweet!

Now you're married we wish you joy,
First the girl, and then the boy.
Kiss her once, kiss her twice,
Kiss her three times over!

Ring-a-ring o'roses,
A pocket full of posies,
 A-tishoo! A-tishoo!
We all fall down.

The cows are in the meadow
Lying fast asleep,
 A-tishoo! A-tishoo!
We all get up again.

Here we go round the Mulberry Bush

Here we go round the mulberry bush,
The mulberry bush, the mulberry bush,
Here we go round the mulberry bush,
On a cold and frosty morning.

This is the way we wash our hands,
Wash our hands, wash our hands,
This is the way we wash our hands,
On a cold and frosty morning.

This is the way we wash our clothes,
Wash our clothes, wash our clothes,
This is the way we wash our clothes,
On a cold and frosty morning.

This is the way we go to school,
Go to school, go to school,
This is the way we go to school,
On a cold and frosty morning.

This is the way we come out of school,
Come out of school, come out of school,
This is the way we come out of school,
On a cold and frosty morning.

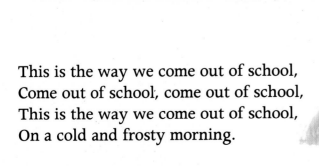

Winter songs

The north wind doth blow,
And we shall have snow,
And what will poor Robin do then?
 Poor thing.
He'll sit in a barn,
And keep himself warm,
And hide his head under his wing,
 Poor thing.

Button to chin
When October comes in.
Cast not a clout
Till May be out.

Cuckoo, cuckoo, cherry tree,
Catch a bird, and give it me;
Let the tree be high or low,
Let it hail or rain or snow.

Snow, snow faster,
Ally-ally-blaster;
The old woman's plucking her geese,
Selling the feathers a penny a piece.

Jingle, bells! jingle, bells!
Jingle all the way:
Oh, what fun it is to ride
In a one-horse open sleigh.

Christmas time

Little Jack Horner
Sat in the corner,
Eating a Christmas pie;
He put in his thumb,
And pulled out a plum,
And said, What a good boy am I!

God bless the master of this house
  And its good mistress too,
And all the little children
  That round the table go;
And all your kin and kinsmen,
  That dwell both far and near;
We wish you a merry Christmas
  And a happy New Year.

Merry are the bells, and merry would they ring,
Merry was myself, and merry could I sing;
With a merry ding-dong, happy, gay, and free,
And a merry sing-song, happy let us be.

Christmas is coming,
    The geese are getting fat,
Please put a penny
    In the old man's hat.
If you haven't got a penny,
    A ha'penny will do;
If you haven't got a ha'penny,
    Then God bless you!

Hush Little Baby

Hush, little baby, don't say a word,
Papa's going to buy you a mocking bird.

If the mocking bird won't sing,
Papa's going to buy you a diamond ring.

If the diamond ring turns to brass,
Papa's going to buy you a looking-glass.

If the looking-glass gets broke,
Papa's going to buy you a billy-goat.

If that billy-goat runs away,
Papa's going to buy you another today.

Time for bed . . .

Boys and girls come out to play,
The moon doth shine as bright as day.
Leave your supper and leave your sleep,
And join your playfellows in the street.
Come with a whoop and come with a call,
Come with a good will or not at all.
Up the ladder and down the wall,
A half-penny loaf will serve us all;
You find milk, and I'll find flour,
And we'll have a pudding in half an hour.

Wee Willie Winkie runs through the town,
Upstairs and downstairs in his night-gown,
Rapping at the window, crying through the lock,
Are all the children in their beds, for now it's eight o'clock?

Jack be nimble,
Jack be quick,
Jack jump over
The candlestick.

Twinkle, twinkle, little star,
How I wonder what you are!
Up above the world so high,
Like a diamond in the sky.

Notes for parents and teachers

Collins English Nursery Rhymes is a beautifully illustrated collection of nearly 100 rhymes, chants and singing games. These rhymes have been sung, said and played to by English-speaking children for many generations and still form a part of every English-speaking child's upbringing.

Most children enjoy singing together or playing rhythmical games in their own language. The rhythm of the verses helps children build up fluency, and the presence of rhyming words helps them to concentrate on pronunciation. Children who are brought up with songs and stories will benefit from a wider vocabulary and a greater confidence in using their own language. The same can be said of learning a second language. Have you noticed how teenagers learn the words of their favourite pop songs *very* quickly, although the same words in a course book would have created much less enthusiasm? Young children will react to the nursery rhymes in the same way.

By using the cassette they find it easy and enjoyable to listen to the singing and the rhythm of the chants, and soon they will find that they can join in. Even if their initial understanding of the words is poor, they can understand the general theme of the rhyme by looking at the illustrations, and parents and teachers can always give a brief, approximate translation. Once children are able to join in confidently with the cassette they will feel a great sense of achievement – singing or chanting rhymes is something they can do as well in English as in their own language.

Music

The cassette should be regarded as the main teaching aid. It has been professionally recorded using children's voices, with particular attention given to making the words clear.

The melody line of songs is printed at the back of the book, along with basic guitar chords, for those who wish to accompany the songs themselves. However, as teachers need to give their pupils full attention while leading them in singing and action games, it is suggested that only confident musicians should attempt to accompany the children. Most teachers and parents would be advised to use the cassette or to sing unaccompanied. Also printed alongside the music are details of how to play some of the better-known games.

Children enjoy adding simple, untuned percussion, i.e. drums, shakers, bells, woodblocks, tambourines etc. – whatever is available or can be improvised. Many children may have such simple instruments at home, if there are none available in class, or they could enjoy making their own. Children can often be quite creative in thinking up alternative percussive 'sound-makers', and teachers should allow them some freedom in deciding what sounds might be appropriate for a particular song or chant.

If there are no instruments available, the children can use their bodies to keep the beat, i.e. clapping, slapping knees, marching feet etc. Indeed miming the rhymes while singing will help the process of memorisation, and add to the enjoyment, as children like to participate with their whole body.

Notes for parents

Parents can help their children gain confidence in using the English language simply by playing the cassette for listening enjoyment, just as they might enjoy a similar cassette in their own language.

Parents (and teachers) need not worry if their English or music skills are not very great. The cassette alone will teach music, pronunciation and intonation and parents can use the written rhymes to check unknown vocabulary and to give a general translation.

Children are usually uninhibited about singing in public and, given a little encouragement, will join in with the music after two or three hearings. Perhaps the best encouragement a child can get is to see his or her parent enthusiastically trying to sing along with the cassette. If you do this, however, it is preferable not to read the words for the first few hearings as pronunciation is better learnt by ear than by eye!

Use the book and cassette imaginatively, according to the age of your child. Looking at the book while listening to the cassette can be a quiet activity, e.g. at bedtime, or on a long journey. It can be a noisy, cheerful activity at home, miming to the action songs with parents or brothers and sisters, skipping round the room, or marching along banging a home-made drum.

The essential factor is that the children should enjoy the rhymes. It is surprising how much children enjoy repeating songs and games without becoming bored. If they find it fun to sing along to the cassette then they will want to listen to it again and again.

Notes for teachers

As explained above, the essential factor in using songs and games in teaching English is that the children should have fun. Once enjoyment has gone the whole purpose of them is lost.

When to use

Obviously the amount of rhymes covered at one time will vary according to the age and ability of the pupils, and the time available. Teachers will develop their own way of incorporating them into a regular English course, but the three main ways are as follows:

1   To bring light relief to more formal work.
2   As a musical session, combining language learning with physical activity.
3   To illustrate a particular teaching point (usually this will happen after the rhyme is well-known to pupils).

For instance a substitution exercise could be done with *Lavender's blue*, to practise the names of colours. You sing:
'Lavender's blue, diddle, diddle,
Lavender's <u>queen</u> ...' (or any word rhyming with 'green'.)
Ask the children to listen for your mistake and to tell you the right colour word. Next, sing the same two lines again, this time substituting 'green' with another word that rhymes with say, 'red', e.g. 'bed'. Ask the children to tell you the name for a colour that rhymes with 'bed', and so on with the other primary colours.

It would be a good idea to have large cards available of each colour to hold up as you say the rhymed word.

A starting point for an activity dealing with what things are made of could be the rhyme *What are little boys made of?*
Point to something in the classroom, e.g. books. Ask the question: 'What are books made of?' The children answer: 'Paper!'

Now split the group in two. Explain that group A will ask the question and group B will answer. Point to books again. When they have performed the task correctly it is group A's turn to ask. Point to something else: windows, walls, etc. Alternatively, you can prepare cards representing things which cannot be found in a classroom. The children work in pairs: each

has a different pile of cards. In turn they ask the question and answer. Each good answer scores a point!

Suggestions on teaching

Unlike parents, who can learn alongside their children, teachers should make sure they have a thorough knowledge of the music, mimes and useful vocabulary before introducing new rhymes to their pupils. They also need to be aware that some phrases are nonsensical, but fun to say, i.e. 'ickle, ockle, blue bockle', or old-fashioned, i.e. 'thirteen, fourteen, maids a-courting'. This can be briefly explained to the children and should not create any difficulties. Being traditional rhymes they are not graded according to difficulty, but simply grouped by subject matter (usually one subject per double-page spread).

The following is one way in which teachers could introduce the rhymes to their pupils:

1   Give a brief translation of the general heading and subject matter of a small section, e.g. all rhymes on one spread. Let the children hear them 2 or 3 times.
2   Give a more detailed translation for one rhyme and suggest certain key words that the children should listen for. (Discourage reading of words until they are well-known.) Let the children join in with the teacher as much as possible – initially by swaying to the rhythm, beating time or miming the actions – and soon the words will follow. At this point, it may help if the teacher asks the children to repeat the rhyme after him, slowly, line by line.
3   Only when the pupils can chant or sing the rhyme off by heart should the teacher attempt to play the group games, e.g. *Here we go round the Mulberry Bush*, or add any percussion instruments (apart from body sounds). Indeed, the promise of a game, or instruments to play, can be used as an added incentive to learning a rhyme more quickly, providing this does not take away from the children's enjoyment.

Summary

Obviously teachers' time and resources vary considerably and the above notes should be recognised as suggestions only. However, the more imagination that a teacher or parent can put into making the nursery rhymes enjoyable, the more their children will willingly repeat them and learn from them. When you see a group of children playing *Oranges and lemons* or some other English game, in their free time, you will know you have succeeded in making the English language come alive!
Rosie Green, February 1986

Music and vocabulary notes

Note to musicians

Where chords are marked with a 7th (C7, A7 etc) it is sufficient to play the straight chord (C, A etc).

Let's Begin, p. 4

Out goes the rat; Dip, dip, dip; Ickle, ockle, blue, bockle; Eenie, meenie, minie, mo   These are all chants used to choose someone as leader or 'it' for a game. One child stands in the centre of the circle and points to each child in turn while reciting the chant. When the last word is reached the child being pointed at is 'out'. The counting-out continues until only one child remains who is then 'it'.

One potato, two potato   In this, the children hold out both fists (or potatoes) to be counted separately so each one has two chances before he is out.

One to ten, and then again, p. 6

One to ten, and then again   For hundreds of years children have learned to count by means of rhymes.

One, two, three   A skipping rhyme.

One, two, three, four, five   A finger-play game.

One, two, buckle my shoe   A counting rhyme with actions
to delve = to dig
a-courting = attracting boy or girl friends

Nursery days, p. 8

PAT-A-CAKE, PAT-A-CAKE

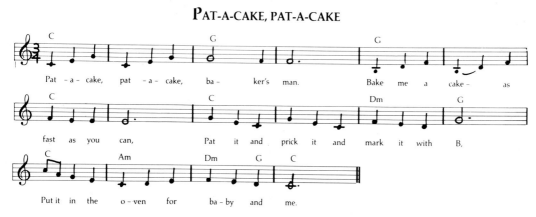

Clapping and hand-action song. First clap hands, then stir the cake, shape it and draw a letter 'B' on the baby's hand. Finally throw the cake vigorously into the oven and clap rhythmically to the end of the song.

Bye, baby bunting   A rocking lullaby.
bye = sleep
baby bunting = short, plump baby

DANCE TO YOUR DADDY

Baby's bouncing song.
babby, fishy = childish forms of baby, fish
rattle basket = rattle made of basket work.

54

Hush-a-bye baby on the tree top   A lullaby.
hush-a-bye = sleep quietly

How many days has my baby to play?   A rhyme for the days of the week.

Nonsensical rhymes, p. 10

RUB-A-DUB-DUB

rub-a-dub =rub, as in washing clothes
'twas = it was

Rub - a - dub - dub, Three men in a tub, And how do you think they got

there? The bu - tcher the ba - ker, The can - dle stick ma - ker, They

all jumped out of a rot - ten po - ta - to,

(spoken) "Twas enough to make a man stare."

HEY DIDDLE, DIDDLE

diddle = nonsense word
fiddle = violin

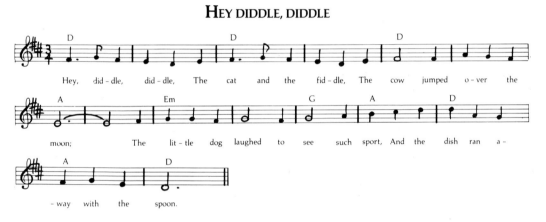

Hey, did - dle, did - dle, The cat and the fid - dle, The cow jumped o - ver the

moon; The lit - tle dog laughed to see such sport, And the dish ran a -

- way with the spoon.

A man in the wilderness, he asked me   An old riddle.

Humpty Dumpty sat on the wall   An action song.

Owen Moore went away   A play on words that sound similar, but have different meanings.

Hoddley, poddley, puddle and fogs   A rhythmic nonsense chant.

Mother, may I go out to swim?   hickory limb = branch of a hickory tree (North American walnut)

In the City, in the street, p. 12

London Bridge is falling down   A singing game. This has been sung all over Europe since the Middle Ages. It was played like *Oranges and lemons*.

Up and down the City Road   An action song, skipping and jumping.
The Eagle = an inn; tuppence = twopenny; pop = pawn; weasel = a hat maker's tool. This refers to the old custom of hatters pawning (selling) their tools over the weekend to buy drink or food.

Oranges and lemons   A singing game. Two children are chosen to form an arch with their hands and secretly decide who will be 'oranges' and who 'lemons'. The rest of the children dance round and round through the arch while they sing to the end of the song. The two children forming the arch then move their hands up and down like a chopper as the rest hurry through the arch to avoid being caught and they all chant: 'Here comes a candle to light you to bed, And here comes a chopper to chop off your head, Chip, chop, chip, chop, last man's dead!'. The last child passing through at the end of the chant is caught between the arms of the chopper. She is asked if she will choose 'oranges' or 'lemons' and she gives her answer in whispers so that the rest cannot know which side she has chosen. She then stands behind her chosen side and the song starts again. When all the children are caught, the two sides have a tug-of-war to see which can pull the other side over.

Sally go round the sun   A playground song. The children link hands and spin round in a circle as they sing.

Mary had a little lamb, p. 14

MARY HAD A LITTLE LAMB

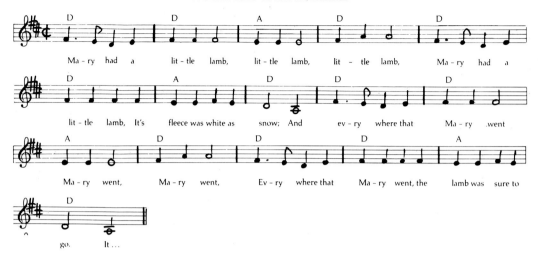

Ma – ry had a lit – tle lamb, lit – tle lamb, lit – tle lamb, Ma – ry had a

lit – tle lamb, It's fleece was white as snow; And ev – ry where that Ma – ry .went

Ma – ry went, Ma – ry went, Ev – ry where that Ma – ry went, the lamb was sure to

go. It . . .

Down on the farm, p. 16

Come, butter come An ancient charm used to speed up
butter-making.

LITTLE BO-PEEP

Lit – tle Bo – peep has lost her sheep, And does – n't know where to find them; Leave them a – lone, and

they'll come home, Bringing their tails – be – hind them.

Cherry stone rhymes, p. 18
These are rhymes used by children to tell their
fortunes by counting cherry stones or by skipping.

What's for dinner? p. 20

Pease porridge hot A clapping song to warm cold hands.
Two children stand facing each other and clap hands to
the rhythm of the song in this way: clap own hands,
clap right hands, own hands, left hands, own hands,
both hands then start again, own hands, right hands
and so on. They clap faster and faster until someone
makes a mistake.

LITTLE MISS MUFFET

tuffet = grassy
mound
curds and whey =
milky cheese

Lit – tle Miss Muffet Sat on a tuf – fet, Eat – ing her curds and whey; There came a big spider, Who

sat down be – side her And fright – ened Miss Muffet a – way.

LITTLE TOMMY TUCKER

e'er = ever or even

Lit – tle Tom – my Tuck – er Sings for his supper: What shall we give him? White bread and but – ter.

How shall he cut it With – out e'er a knife – How will he be mar – ried With – out e'er a wife?

JACK SPRAT

platter = flat dish

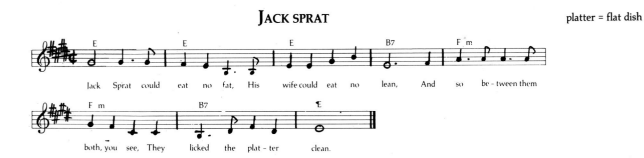

Jack Sprat could eat no fat, His wife could eat no lean, And so be – tween them

both, you see, They licked the plat – ter clean.

Jack and Jill, p. 22

crown = head
caper = run and jump

Jack and Jill Went up the hill, To fetch a pail of wa – ter; Jack fell down, And

broke his crown, And Jill came tumb – ling af – ter.

Rain, rain go away, p. 24

Rain, rain go away One of many old chants used by children to charm the rain away.

IPSEY WIPSEY SPIDER

A finger action song. The thumbs touch opposite little fingers while the hands rotate back and forth, to show the spider climbing up the spout.

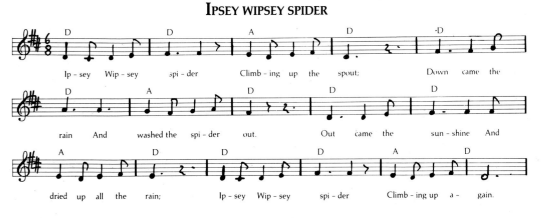

Ip – sey Wip – sey spi – der Climb – ing up the spout; Down came the

rain And washed the spi – der out. Out came the sun – shine And

dried up all the rain; Ip – sey Wip – sey spi – der Climb – ing up a – gain.

Lazy days, p. 26

LADYBIRD, LADYBIRD

Lad – y bird, lad – y bird, Fly a – way home, Your house is on fire – And your

chil – dren are gone; All ex – cept one – And that's lit – tle Ann – And

she has crept un – der The fry – ing pan.

A magic rhyme known all over Europe. The ladybird is put on the child's finger and the rhyme sung. Then the child blows on the ladybird and it will usually fly away.

A diller, a dollar   Probably means slow and stupid boy.   *The cock's on the woodpile*   a-threshing = threshing

LITTLE BOY BLUE

Lit – tle Boy Blue, Come blow your horn, The sheep's in the mead – ow, The

cow's in the corn. Where's the boy Who looks af – ter the sheep? He's

un – der the hay – cock Fast a – sleep. Will you wake him?

No, not I, For if I do – He's sure to cry. –

Playtime, p. 28

LUCY LOCKET

Lu – cy Lo – cket lost her poc – ket, Kit – ty Fish – er found it; Not a pen – ny

was there in it, On – ly rib – bon round it.

pocket = purse
One child stands blind-fold in the middle of a circle of children. A second child walks slowly around the outside of the circle while they all sing the song. After the end he continues around and quietly drops an object behind one of the children in the ring, who has to try to catch the dropper before he runs round the

circle and gets back to where he dropped it. If he can do this, he then changes places with the dropper and the game starts again. However, if the blindfolded child can guess where the object was dropped while the children are chasing each other, then he changes places with the dropper and the game continues.

Strange folk, p. 30

GOOSEY GOOSEY GANDER

goosey = goose
chamber = bedroom

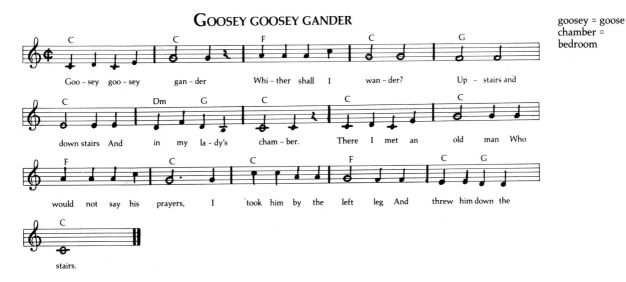

Goo-sey goo-sey gan-der Whi-ther shall I wan-der? Up-stairs and down stairs And in my la-dy's cham-ber. There I met an old man Who would not say his prayers, I 'took him by the left leg And threw him down the stairs.

THERE WAS A CROOKED MAN

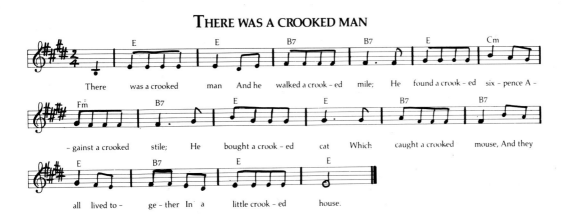

There was a crooked man And he walked a crook-ed mile; He found a crook-ed six-pence A-gainst a crooked stile; He bought a crook-ed cat Which caught a crooked mouse, And they all lived to-ge-ther In a little crook-ed house.

THERE WAS AN OLD WOMAN

quoth = said
aye, by-an-by = yes, very soon

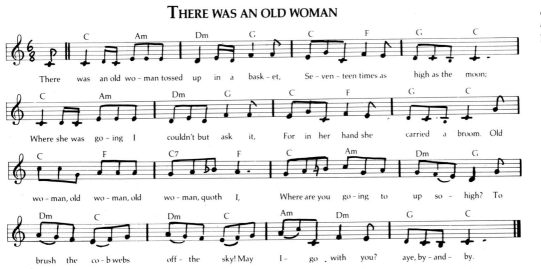

There was an old wo-man tossed up in a bask-et, Se-ven-teen times as high as the moon; Where she was go-ing I couldn't but ask it, For in her hand she carried a broom. Old wo-man, old wo-man, old wo-man, quoth I, Where are you go-ing to up so high? To brush the co-b webs off the sky! May I go with you? aye, by-and-by.

DR FOSTER WENT TO GLOUCESTER

Doc - tor Fos - ter went to Glouce - ster In a show - er of rain; He stepped in a puddle, Right

up to his mid - dle, And ne - ver went there a - gain.

Soldier, Soldier, p. 32

SOLDIER, SOLDIER

musket = gun
fife = flute

Oh sol - dier, sol - dier, will you mar - ry me With your musk - et fife and drum? Oh,

no, pret - ty maid, I can - not mar - ry you For I have no coat to put on. Then a -

way she went To her grand fa - ther's chest And brought him one of the ver - y ver - y best And the

sol - dier put it on. Oh, sol - dier, sol - dier, will you mar - ry me With your

musket fife and drum? Oh no, pret - ty maid, I can - not mar - ry you For I

have no socks to put on. Then a - ...

Kings and Queens, p. 34

OLD KING COLE

fiddle = violin

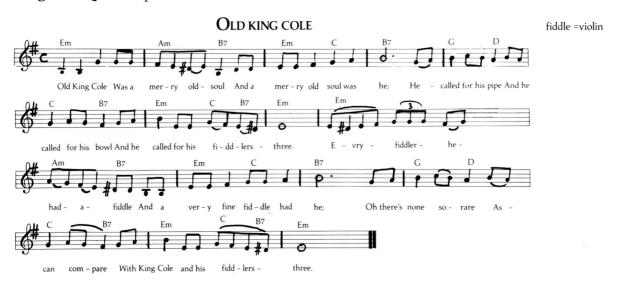

Old King Cole Was a mer - ry old - soul And a mer - ry old soul was he; He - called for his pipe And he

called for his bowl And he called for his fi - dd - lers - three. E - vry - fiddler - he -

had - a - fiddle And a ver - y fine fid - dle had he; Oh there's none so - rare As -

can com - pare With King Cole and his fidd - lers - three.

60

LAVENDER'S BLUE

diddle, diddle =
nonsense words

La-ven-der's blue did-dle, did-dle, La-ven-der's green; When I am king, did-dle, did-dle,

You shall be queen.

Bow-wow says the dog, p. 36

MY LITTLE DOG

Oh where, oh where has my lit-tle dog gone? Oh where oh where can he

be? With his ears cut short and his tail cut long, Oh

where oh where is he?

Join hands, p. 38

POOR MARY LIES A-WEEPING

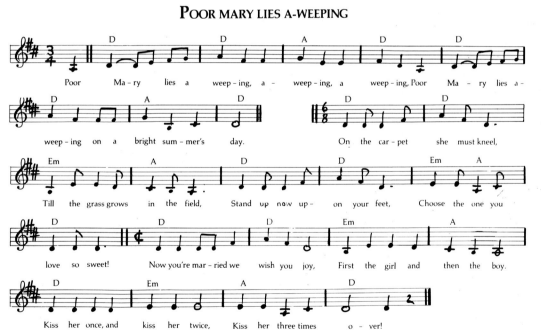

Poor Ma-ry lies a weep-ing, a weep-ing, a weep-ing, Poor Ma-ry lies a-

weep-ing on a bright sum-mer's day. On the car-pet she must kneel,

Till the grass grows in the field, Stand up now up- on your feet, Choose the one you

love so sweet! Now you're mar-ried we wish you joy, First the girl and then the boy.

Kiss her once, and kiss her twice, Kiss her three times o - ver!

Action song. The
children dance in a
circle, singing,
while Mary kneels
in the centre,
weeping. They
stand still while
Mary chooses one
of them to come
to the centre and
kisses him three
times over. Then
the chosen child
becomes Mary and
the song starts
again. Note the
change in tempo.

RING A RING O' ROSES

o'roses = of roses
posies = small
bunches of
flowers
a-tishoo = sound
of a sneeze.

Ring - a - ring o' - ros - es, A pock - et full of pos - ies A - tish - oo! a-

-tish - oo! We all fall down. The cows are in the mea-dow Ly-ing fast a-

-sleep, A - tish - oo! a - tish - oo! We all get up a - gain.

The children dance around in a circle then stop to sneeze and all fall down and so on.

Little love ditties, p. 40

CURLY LOCKS

Cur - ly locks Cur - ly locks wilt thou be mine? Thou shalt not wash dishes Nor

yet feed the swine; But sit on a cush - ion And sew a fine seam, And

feed up - on straw - ber - ries Su - gar and cream.

wilt thou = will you
thou shalt = you shall
nor yet = also not
swine = pigs

WHAT ARE LITTLE BOYS MADE OF?

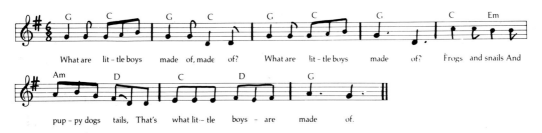

What are lit - tle boys made of, made of? What are lit - tle boys made of? Frogs and snails And

pup - py dogs tails, That's what lit - tle boys - are made of.

One I love; She loves me; He loves me   These are children's
rhymes used to guess their future while throwing a
handful of stones or petals from a flower, one by one.

Here we go round the Mulberry Bush, p. 42

HERE WE GO ROUND THE MULBERRY BUSH

Here we go round the mul - 'bry bush, The mul 'bry bush, the mul - 'bry bush, Here we go round the

mul - 'bry bush, On a cold and frosty morn - ing.

An action song. The children dance in a circle, holding hands, and then stop for the action verses. Each action verse should be followed by a vigorous circle dance, singing round the mulberry bush.

Winter songs, p. 44

THE NORTH WIND DOTH BLOW

The north wind doth blow, - And we shall have snow, And what will poor

doth = does

Ro – bin do then? Poor thing. He'll sit in a barn, – And keep himself

warm, And' hide his head un – der his wing, Poor thing.

Button to chin   Cast not a clout = Do not take off
(winter) clothing

Snow, snow faster   ally-blaster = strong wind (possible
meaning)

JINGLE BELLS, JINGLE BELLS

Jin – gle, bells! jin – gle, bells! Jin – gle all the way: Oh, what fun it is to ride In a

one – horse o – pen sleigh. Jin – gle, bells! jin – gle, bells! Jin – gle all the way:

Oh, what fun it is to ride In a one – horse o – pen sleigh!

Christmas time, p. 46

LITTLE JACK HORNER

Lit – tle Jack Hor – ner Sat in a cor – ner, Eat – ing a Christ – mas pie; He put in his thumb, And

pulled out a plum, And said, what a good boy am I!

CHRISTMAS IS COMING

ha'penny =
halfpenny

Christ – mas is com – ing, The geese are get – ting fat, Please put a

pen – ny In the old man's hat. If you hav – n't got a pen – ny, A

ha' – pen – ny will do; If you haven't got a ha' – penny, Then God bless

you!

Hush Little Baby, p. 48

HUSH LITTLE BABY

billy-goat = male goat

Hush, lit-tle ba-by, don't say a word, Pa-pa's going to buy you a mock-ing - bird.

If the mock-ing bird won't sing, Pa-pa's going to buy you a dia-mond ring.

Time for bed, p. 50

BOYS AND GIRLS COME OUT TO PLAY

doth = does

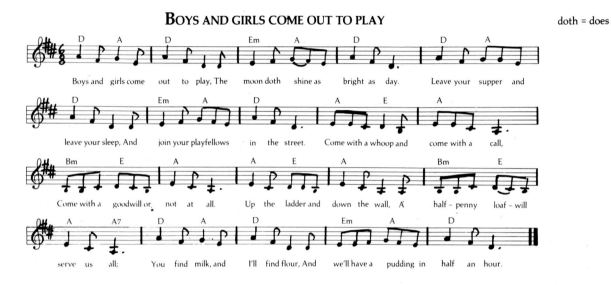

Boys and girls come out to play, The moon doth shine as bright as day. Leave your supper and

leave your sleep, And join your playfellows in the street. Come with a whoop and come with a call,

Come with a goodwill or not at all. Up the ladder and down the wall, A half - penny loaf - will

serve us all; You find milk, and I'll find flour, And we'll have a pudding in half an hour.

WEE WILLIE WINKIE

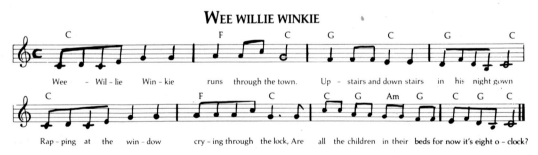

Wee - Wil-lie Win-kie runs through the town. Up - stairs and down stairs in his night gown

Rap-ping at the win-dow cry-ing through the lock, Are all the children in their beds for now it's eight o - clock?

TWINKLE, TWINKLE, LITTLE STAR

Twin-kle, twin-kle lit-tle star How I won-der what you are! Up a-bove the

world so high, - like a dia-mond in the sky, - Twin-kle, twin-kle lit-tle star,

How I won-der what you are.